T0068457

Copyright © 2019 by Crayola

Copyright © 2019 by Crayola

Copyright © 2019 by Crayola

Copyright © 2019 by Crayola

Copyright © 2019 by Crayola

Copyright © 2019 by Crayola

Copyright © 2019 by Crayola

Copyright © 2019 by Crayola

Crayola
My First Big Sticker Book
BuzzPop

Stars in Space

Help the spaceship travel to its home planet. How many stars does it pass along the way?

ANSWER: ____

Answer on Page 63

Pond Pals

Find the stickers to complete this scene.

Ship, Ahoy!

Find two more pirate ships on your sticker sheets. Add them to the scene, so the pirates can trade treasure.

Time for T. rex

Can you make this giant dinosaur colorful?

Winter *Whoosh!*

Find the numbered stickers for this page. Then match them to the picture so the penguin can glide!

Answer on Page 63

Unicorn

Fairy

Mermaid

Pegasus

Magical Matching

Draw a line to match each magical creature to its name.

Answers on Page 63

Move Your Body

These friends like to exercise together. Find the correct sticker to complete each pattern.

Answers on Page 63

Starry Night

What a beautiful night sky! How many stars do you see?

Your answer: _____

Answer on Page 63

Busy Yard

Use your stickers to add a bird, a bug, a snail, a skunk, and a worm to this scene.

Woof!

Draw a silly face on the balloon puppy.
Then color it to make it your own.

Answer on Page 63

Buzzz!

These busy bees are working on their hive. How many can you count?

Answer on Page 63

Your answer: _____

Cock-a-doodle-doo!

Color the picture. Then use your stickers to add one hen and two baby chicks to the farm.

So Many Monkeys

Circle the one that's upside down, and color the rest that are hanging around.

Answer on Page 63

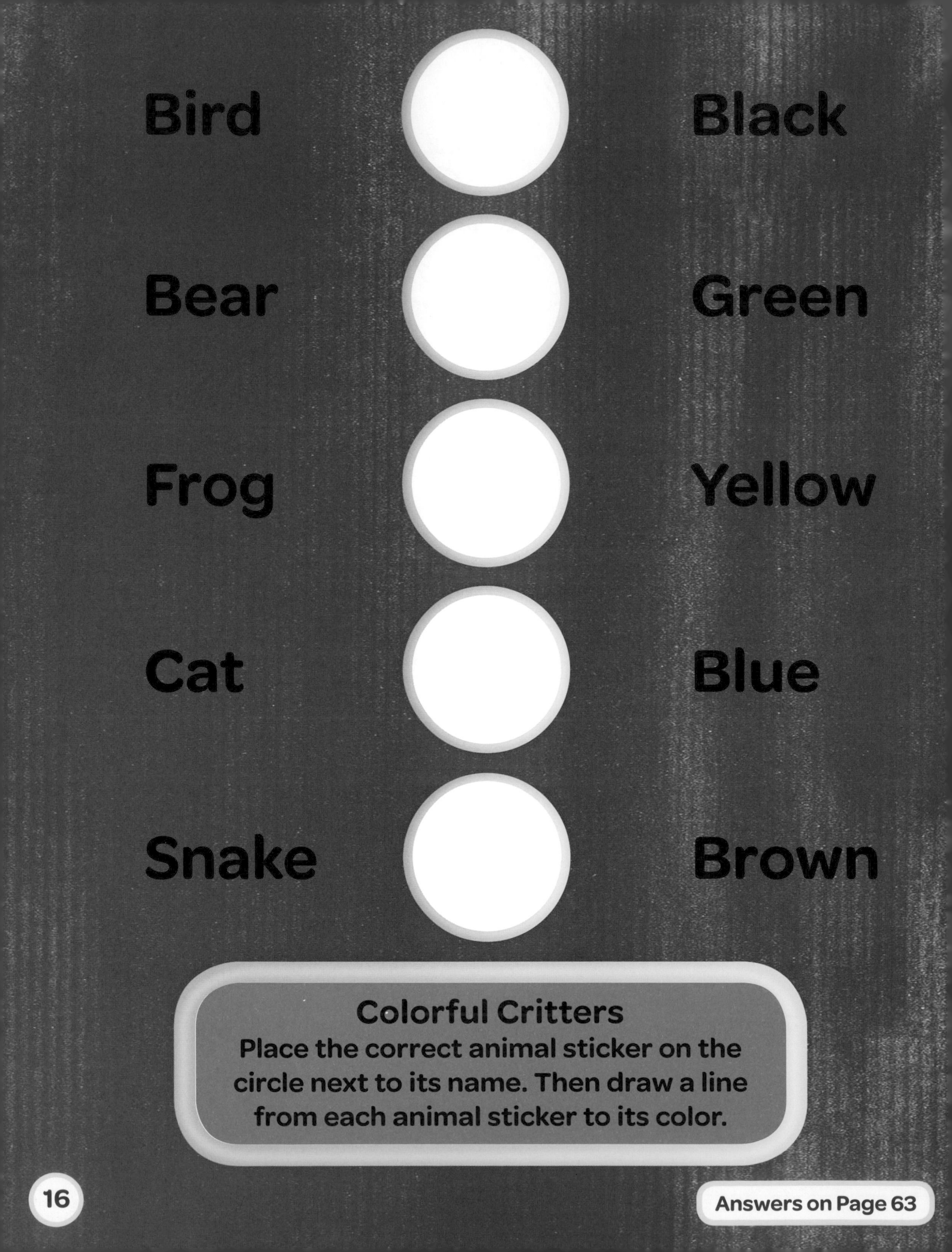

Bird

Bear

Frog

Cat

Snake

Black

Green

Yellow

Blue

Brown

Colorful Critters

Place the correct animal sticker on the circle next to its name. Then draw a line from each animal sticker to its color.

Answers on Page 63

Snow Day!

Oops! Something is missing. Find the numbered stickers for this page. Then match them to the picture so the friends can zoom down the hill.

Answer on Page 63

Autumn!

It's time for leaves to fall off trees.
Can you count them?

How many are on the branches? _____

How many are falling down? _____

How many are on the ground? _____

Answers on Page 63

Stripes and Spots

Oh, no! The zebra and giraffe have lost their patterns! Can you color them in?

Under the Sea

Trace this fish along the dashed outlines. Then color it any way you wish!

Barnyard Buddies

It's a busy day on the farm. Find the animal stickers to complete this scene.

Happy Birthday!

Today is a special day. Use the dots as a color guide to create a yummy cake.

On a Mission!

Use your stickers to give the astronaut some planets to discover.

Yo-ho-ho!
Find three jewels and one crown on your sticker sheets, and put them in the treasure chest.

I Spy a Candy Shop

This store is filled with yummy treats. Make four gumballs green, two lollipops yellow, and one cupcake pink. Then color the rest however you want.

Hungry for Books!

Help this worm eat its way through the apple to find some more books.

Answer on Page 63

Monkey See, Monkey Eat!

Find the numbered stickers for this page. Then match them to the picture to give the monkey a treat.

Answer on Page 63

Fall Season

Circle the scene that is a little different.

Answer on Page 64

Sundae, Fun Day

Find the banana split sticker and place it on the circle. Then color the sundae to match the sticker.

Deep in the Ocean

These sea creatures are waiting for their buddies. Add stickers for a whale, a seahorse, and a jellyfish, so they can go for a swim together.

Silly Monster!
Can you make this monster's fur look funny and special?

Snow Puppy

This little doggie loves to play in the snow. How many snowballs does he have?

The dog has _____ snowballs.

Answer on Page 64

Who says "Quack"?
Connect the dots to find out.

Answer on Page 64

You Can Do It!

Help the cow jump over the moon. Use your stickers to complete the puzzle.

Great Job!

You just won a trophy! Write your name on it.

Hooray for Hippos!

Circle the hippo that is a little different. Then color them all.

Answer on Page 64

Nice Kitty!

Connect the dots to see who will grow up to be King of the Jungle!

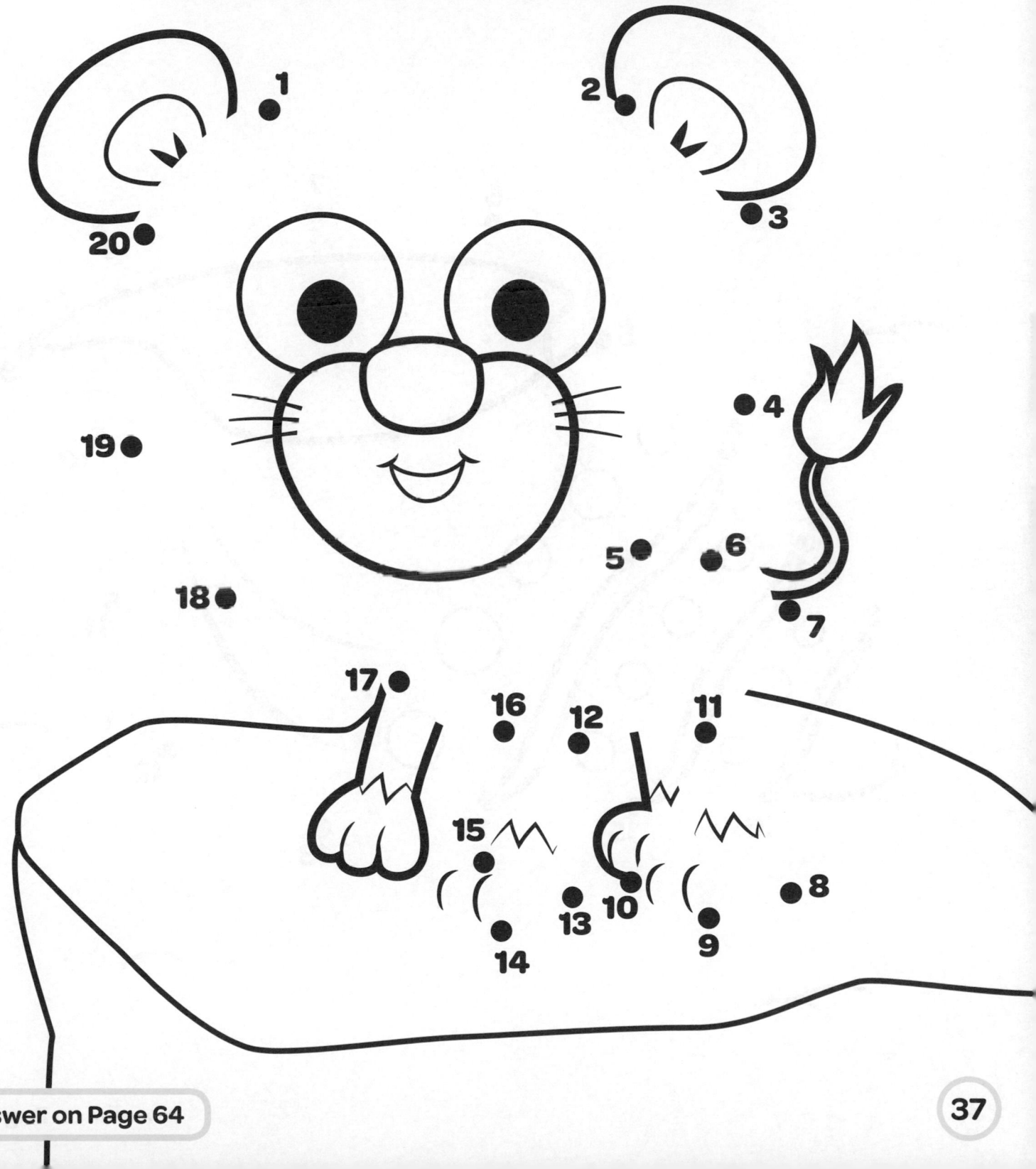

Answer on Page 64

See the Seashell

Connect the dots to find something pretty from the ocean.

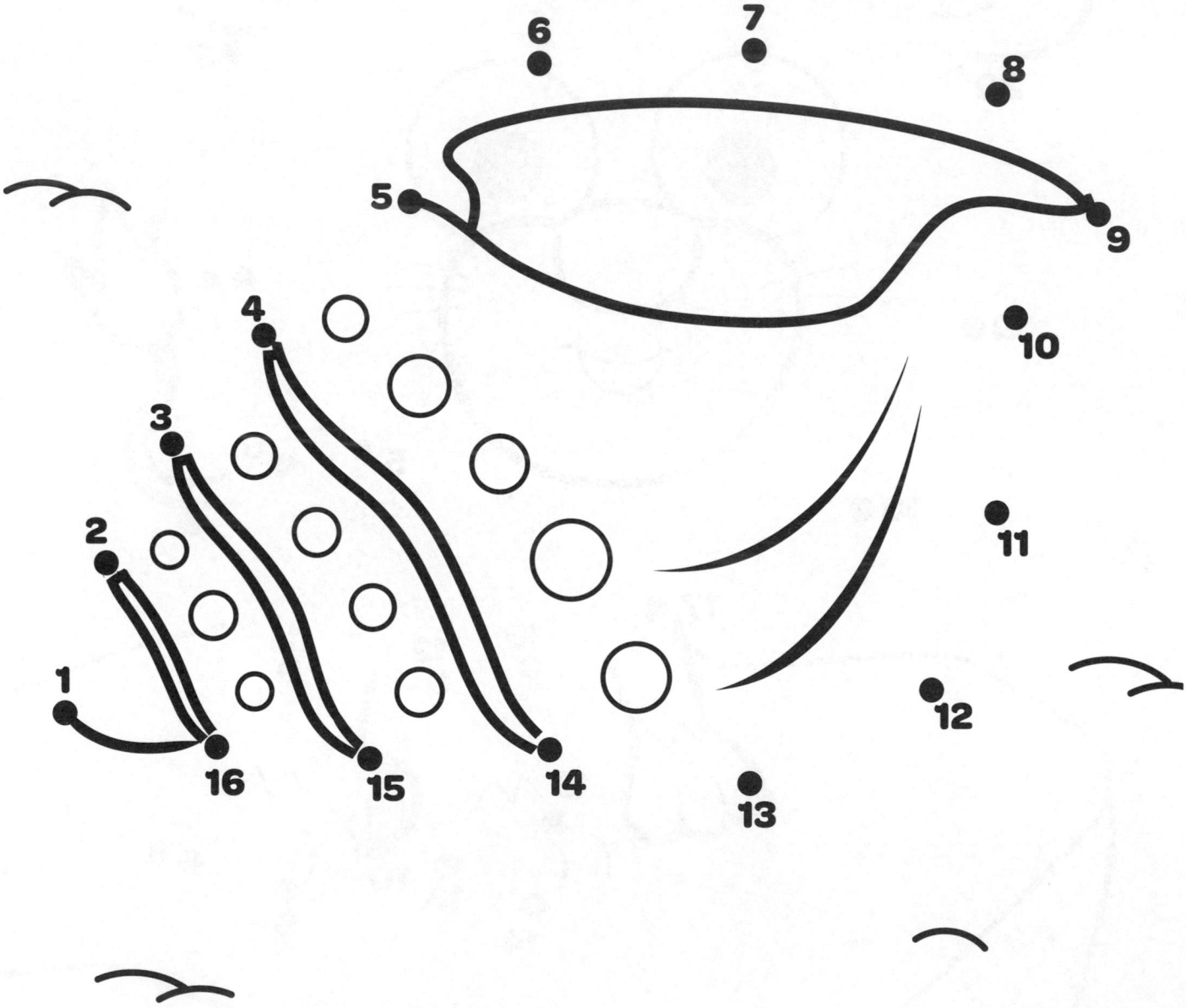

Answer on Page 64

More Bubbles, Please!

This puppy likes his bath extra bubbly. Color the picture and draw as many bubbles as you can on the page.

Flutter, Flutter!

Make each butterfly a different color.

Unicorn Rainbow

Use the dots as a color guide to make this unicorn's rainbow bright!

Pretty Flowers

Can you color the last tulip in each row to complete the pattern?

Answer on Page 64

Friendly Elephant

Trace around the lines of this elephant to complete the picture. Then color it any way you like.

Hungry Rabbit

Find more carrots for the bunny to eat on your sticker sheets.

Smile!

This friendly fairy can make flowers smile. Use your stickers to put a smiling face on both flowers.

Down in the Deep

Circle the submarine that is a little different. Then color them all.

Answer on Page 64

From Caterpillar to Butterfly

This caterpillar will turn into a butterfly one day.
Find four butterfly stickers and place them on the page.

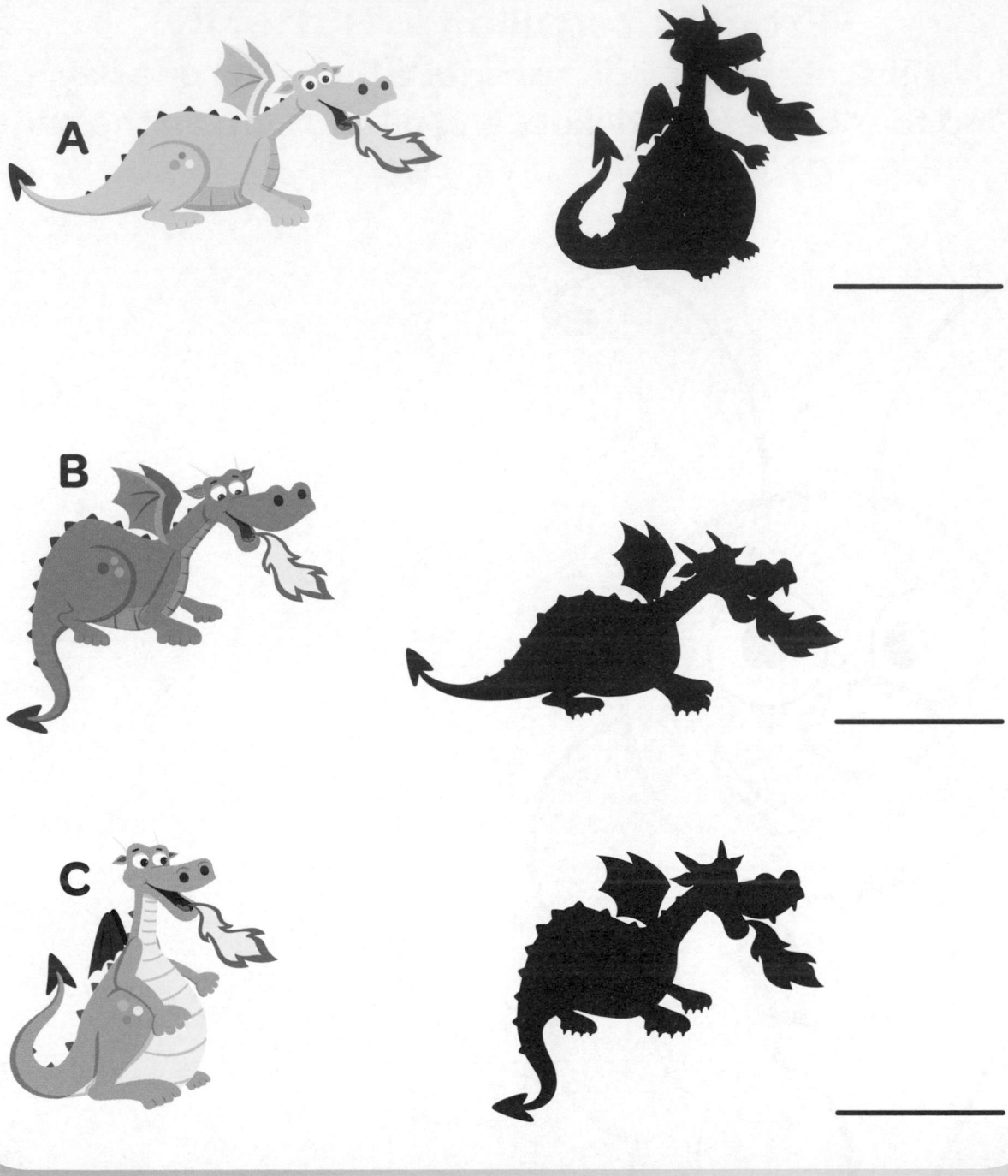

Dragon Shadows

Can you match the dragons to their shadows? Write the correct letter on each line.

Answers on Page 64

Giant Chef

This giant wants to make a fresh apple pie. Use your stickers to add some apples to the tree for him to pick.

Out of This World!

It's almost time to blast off. Finish the drawing so the rocket can soar!

Answer on Page 64

Going Buggy

Trace the lines to finish this cute bug. Then color the picture.

Snow Business

This snowman isn't finished.
Use crayons to give him some color!

A Smiling Shark

How many teeth does this smiling shark have? Color each tooth a different color as you count.

Your answer: _____

Answer on Page 64

Line of Robots

Which robot is the smallest? Which is the biggest? Find your robot stickers and put them in size order.

Just Add Sprinkles

This yummy cupcake is almost ready to eat. Add sprinkle stickers to make it special!

Knight in Shining Armor

The knight can't go to battle dressed like this. Use your stickers to give him his helmet, armor, shield, and sword.

Fly High in the Sky

Color this helicopter red.
Find stickers of more things that fly to add to the page.

Spinning Spider

What kind of web should the spider make? Draw it here.

Go, Go, Go!

Which picture doesn't go with the others? Cross it out.

Answer on Page 64

Lots of Gumballs

Oh, what a lovely gumball machine!
Make one gumball orange, three gumballs blue, four gumballs yellow, and five gumballs green.

Surf's Up!

Use your stickers to decorate the girl's surfboard so she can catch waves in style.

In the Yard

The puppy is looking for his friends. Use your stickers to add a rabbit, a snail, and a bird, so they can play.

Answers

Page 2

The spaceship passes 3 stars.

Page 6

Page 7

Page 8

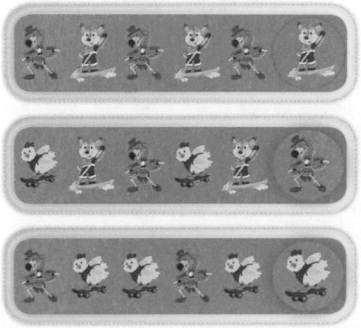

Page 9

There are 5 stars.

Page 12

Page 13

There are 6 bees.

Page 15

Page 16

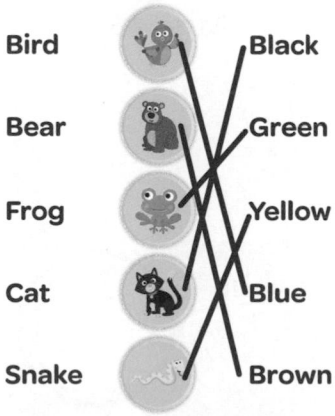

Page 17

Page 18

How many are on the branches? 3

How many are falling down? 1

How many are on the ground? 4

Page 26

Page 27

Answers

Page 28

Page 32

The dog has
7 snowballs.

Page 33

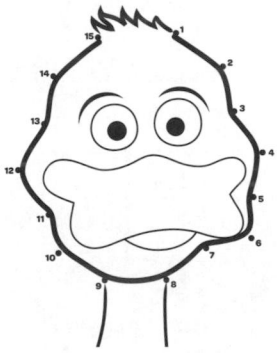

Duck

Page 36

Page 37

Page 38

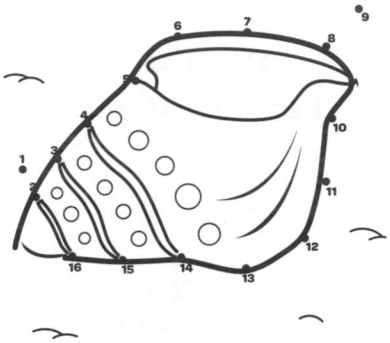

Page 42

Page 46

Page 48

Page 50

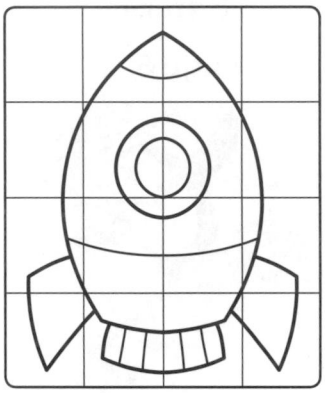

Page 53

The shark has
15 teeth.

Page 59